Of Eyes and Iris

Poems by

Erika Moss Gordon

Liquid Light Press

Premium Chapbook First Edition

ISBN-10: 0988307219

ISBN-13: 978-0-9883072-1-6

Liquid Light Press

poetry that speaks to the heart

www.liquidlightpress.com

Cover Art by Kellie Day

(*kelliedayart.com*)

Cover Design by M. D. Friedman

(*mdfriedman.com*)

Photo of Poet by Brenda K. Colwell

(*brendacolwellphoto.com*)

for my parents, my brother, my children

Contents

Of Eyes and Iris

Linger
at the iris
for one moment longer,

see
how it changes
everything.

By the Ocean

Let's take a walk,
you and I,
to the end of the road
where we will watch
the blue ocean
in all of its chaos
and dependability.
There is nothing
to say really,
except for what we notice
and what we don't,
and if there are words
to describe this love
that crashes
and breaks
over and over again
onto the ever shifting sand,
then let us say those, too.

You Cannot Know

You cannot know
in the time
right before the darkness

when all things
are almost blue,
when the colors are here,

but not
and there is a soft feeling
in the eye

of many fabrics bleeding
together – the aspen grove,
the dusky grass,

the departing wisp
of cloud,
you cannot know

when you walk
alongside the river
to talk about love,

where the geese swim
with their rows of babies
in the eddy

and you stop on a bridge
to watch the shape
of water,

how it fans out white
over the sunken stones
or wrinkles convex,

concave,
you cannot know
and so you don't

and are left standing
grateful
with your blinking eyes

facing into
the center
of things.

Remind Me

Do you want to dance?
Dance.
Do you want to fly?
Fly.
Do you want to breathe?
Breathe.
Do you want to remember everything you know?
Forget.

And Still No Sound from the Bottom

I am
the pebble,
the well,

and the silence.

The Only Way

To fall

in love

with the

world,

fall in

love with

the truth

of yourself.

Highway 550

Into the slate sky,
the edgeless mountains
turned to cloud

astonish our weary eyes
with every blue and grey
on earth,

such whiteness too,
such inexpressible billowing,
that there is nothing

else – no road home,
no driver, no notion
of where we started,

no end.

The Thousand Reasons

Let us set down
the thousand reasons
so that we may finally
speak to the heart
of one another.

Eclipse

I want to write about the sky,
about what happened here tonight,
about the cacophony of birdsong

and then the silence. I want to write
about how the clouds come together
and move apart,

and about how we do the same,
like particles, like golden bits of dust
in a shaft of light. This morning

we tried to catch them
in our hands,
laughing, never sure

of our success,
and I suppose
this is the joy of it – the wondering

the trying, all for the chance
to hold something so delicate
and beautiful,

for even one small moment
and all the while knowing
that as soon as our fingers close

it will be gone.

Hiking in Blaine Basin

Walk into flowers,
into wild waterfalls
and soil soft with living,

where everything,
everything returns
like ashes to water,

pouring from
meadow blossoms
to the deep blue sea -

nothing
left to hold
in a beauty like this.

Of Butterflies

On a dusky road home,
we lift the crepe paper wings
so lifeless, so absolute,

a gift arrives
in orange and black,
two children crouched

in dirt,
pass back and forth
an understanding.

In the Desert

We wandered
to a dusty hillside
.

to see the chards
of ancient pots,

imperfect,
trapezoidal,

so full of sand
and stories,

and that is where
you taught me to see

the beauty
in what is broken.

Definitions

Three things I am:
1. Comfortable in the quiet house
2. Trusting of this heart
3. Confident in the unfolding

Three things I am – also:
1. Uneasy in the quiet house
2. Hesitant of this heart
3. Uncertain in the unfolding

but what is the point
of definitions

when tonight
all that matters

is the way
the sharp,

slender moon
has rocked

into a perfect
white crescent?

We Are Still (Are Always) in the Time of Not Knowing

In the dark hours
of morning,

when there is nothing
between the window

and the mountain,
it is time to rest

into the wide arms
of blackness,

time even to forget
the call of bird

or gracious
break of day.

How long has this candle been out anyway?

Fumbling
through the junk drawer
for a match, I wonder...

At Last (in Spring)

Early blades commence
the green ascent

and our blinking eyes stumble
toward one another again,

squinting in bright yellow,
blue and the warmth

of one thousand
holy promises.

Oh, Yeah

And once again
the shattering
opens the door

to the illusion
that there was
something

to be shattered.

Allowing the Boots

Only the jumper
can determine the perfect
depth of puddle.

What Love Is This?

You have seen the orange lily
turn to face the sun,

and have listened
to tears of farewell

fall beneath the apple tree.
You witnessed a hundred geese

paint triangles across
the sky, calling in concert

with shared ambition, and
watched the snow melt

into the river, into the sea.
But you also met something

dark and formless
that wanted so much

to be love, but could seize
only the wind as it wailed

past your neck and disappeared
over the mountain.

Nine Degrees Fahrenheit

On the coldest
day, why reach
your hand toward
anything but
love?

Three Generations

Unseasonably warm,
but the sidewalk still icy

so we hold each other up

as the snow melts
and refreezes

and melts...

The Five-Year-Old Wants Answers

Tell me again,
what did the fish look like
when it died?

If they called it
The Sinkable, then it wouldn't
have hit the iceberg.

Do you think that
Great Grandma Joanne
is in Lost Vegas?

I want to go up
to outer space to see
all of the babies.

Will a red fox
be under our porch
every spring?

How many of us
will need to throw Pop's ashes?
He was so big.

In the Morning

The first flakes fall
like a rarity,
delicate, earthly
bound, on sallow
grass, whispering
of white blankets
to conceal
late season steel.
Early gossamer
lattice that
will melt
into spring
rivulets, washing
it all away,
leaving nothing but
bare, black earth,
ripe and yearning
for new life to grow.

Law for Letting Go

The weight
of the obstacle

is equal
and opposite to

the intensity
of the holding.

right where you are haiku

stand in the rubble
and realize that your feet
are still on the ground.

Brother

Did
you
know
that
oxygen
can
come
through
the
telephone
line?
I
am
so
grateful
to
be
breathing
again.

Driving. Blizzard.

My wish is for
eighteen more
of you in the
world, says
the five-year-old
to his big sister,

and we sit back
into the sum total
of what we
know.

El Sueño

In the hours between
the rooster and the dog,
where the round rock

balances impossibly,
the Mexican Buddha
watches the horizon,

unwavering in the shadow
of the white breasted
frigate. Still-winged

raven etches black
circles in the salty mist
and is also tattooed

across the back
of the Buddha.
Heron bones swivel

bleached feathers
along the water's edge
calling silently,

burn bright
and return
to the sea.

Parentheses Haiku

Two small bodies curl
into each other, the whole
universe between.

The Fish

listen	I am
more than	a fish
bubbling	swimming
words	around, I am
living	deep
inside of	dark
spaces	between the
silent	oceans.

Under the Broken Branches

Nothing

left to do but lie
on cool pavement

beneath a detonation
of crabapple blossoms

in the blue dome of sky,
each breath opening

to pink.

It Thinks It Owns the Place

Silence in this house
leaves its belongings
scattered in every room
since the last tenant
moved away.

This time, I will try
not to pick up after.

nine lights of restless

1.
the full moon lights
nineteen deer tracks in
the pale yard, this window
needs washing, one side
of this bed no longer needs making.

2.
stringing lights,
the frozen ladder
rocks
back and forth,
back and forth,
on an icy walk,
half shoveled.

3.
do the neighbors notice the time
when the lights go out?

4.
in the city, we swirl martinis
extra dirty beneath blue lights, the bass
shakes our crystal glasses.
we look over the other's shoulder
at our own reflections
in the mirror.

5.

full moon, electric
tides, monitor flashes
into a dark abyss.

6.

last night, a lunar eclipse
while I lay sleeping.

7.

now, when I turn a light on,
it stays on until I turn it off. when I turn
a light off, it stays off until I turn it on.

8.

below fake logs,
the jumpy blue flame
waits for the switch to be thrown.

9.

the refrigerator light squints
and for no reason,
I tiptoe
back to bed.

On the Way Home

Driving down
and down,
a black funnel

beckons behind
each set of lonesome
headlights. Even the white

flustered drifts
cannot survive
against such darkness,

and though the sun
will rise to shine
on these transgressions

murmuring in the dark,
tonight I ride
with shadows

and the road,
it swallows
me whole.

Blossoms

Even as the wild blossoms
send a pink symphony
into the wind so ripe with pollen,

the soil prepares
to take their color back.

On the Banks

The snowmelt drain of river's curve
weaves gently now as summer wanes,
whispering past the algaed rocks
with many treasures lying there.
Our feet plant firmly in the mud,
we watch the wheel turn round again.
Breath rides the breeze to airstream wisps
through crisp orange branches swaying soft,
while green glides quietly away
invited by sly winter dusk.
Why do we stand here on the banks,
even as the birds fly away?

A Crack

A slender opening today
perhaps,
in the company of you
and misted mineral pool.

I think I saw a fish dancing,
it was brilliant,
but it might have been
a stone.

Sea Change

There is something
bubbling, brewing,

calling blue beneath
the surface,

aching,
stirring.

You are listening
and ignoring,

ocean's eager
swells unnerving,

riptides pulling,
unforgiving.

Paddle fast
against the surging

or gaze hard at
what is

churning.
If only you could

quench the wondering,
satisfy the tugging song.

Surrender to depth's
endless calling,

you may find
silence

in the dawn.

Two Questions

#1:
A man
digs a vast hole
in a land where
the ground shakes
from time to time
(the man knows this).
The man
stands at
the precipice.
The earth trembles,
the man
disappears
into the hole.
Whose fault is it?
The ground's,
the hole's,
or
the
man's?

#2:

If another man
witnesses
the fall,
but decides
to dig
his own black hole anyway,
and the earth shakes,
or the pipe breaks,
or the seal leaks,
or the lock creaks,
or the bomb drops,
or the time stops,
then when can
we change
the
man?

About the Author

Poetry began to spill out of Erika Moss Gordon when she was a young child. Today, the themes have changed, but the words are still spilling. *Of Eyes and Iris* is her first book and charts her adult sojourns into landscapes of the vastly unfamiliar and the everyday extraordinary. Erika is a mother, a daughter, a sister, a friend, a lover, a teacher of yoga, a student of life and is, daily, delighted to discover how very little she knows. She lives in Ridgway, Colorado. Her poetry blog, *unlearning through poetry,* is on the web at *erikamossgordon.wordpress.com*.

Credits and Acknowledgements

The following poems originally appeared in the publications listed below:

"Driving. Blizzard." in the "Way of the Mountain #193" article in the *Mountain Gazette Magazine* (November-December, 2012)

"Allowing the Boots Haiku" & "Parentheses Haiku" – *The Telluride Watch*, (March 29, 2012)

"On the Banks"– *Out and About Magazine* (*Grand Junction Daily Sentinel*, December 9, 2011)

"In the Morning" – *Out and About Magazine* (*Grand Junction Daily Sentinel*, March 30, 2012)

Other Books from Liquid Light Press

Leaning Toward Whole, **Poems by M. D. Friedman**
(Released June, 2011)

This poetry chapbook from the international award winning poet, M. D. Friedman, contains pieces both poignant and personal. *Leaning Toward Whole* speaks to both the universal and the everyday, both the moment and the millennium.

The Miracle Already Happening - Everyday Life with Rumi,
Poems by Rosemerry Wahtola Trommer
(Released December, 2011)

Rosemerry Wahtola Trommer's superb collection of poems, inspired by Rumi, is full of heart, humor, peace and wisdom. This chapbook gracefully flings us from our routine into the joy of life, bristles with surprise and dances with mystic vision.

Spiral, **Poems by Lynda La Rocca**
(Released March, 2012)

Award winning poet, Lynda La Rocca, creates a compelling poetic and melodic discourse from the persistent cravings and fears inside of each of us. This book is both as darkly sweet and satisfying as chocolate and as nourishing and healing as mother's chicken soup.

From the Ashes, **Poems by Wayne A. Gilbert**
(Released June , 2012)

Master jazz Sufi poet, Wayne A. Gilbert, chronicles the loss of his mother with powerful, bittersweet honesty to create this beautiful collection of poems that is universal in its scope, transcendent in the depth of its understanding and exquisitely musical in form.

ah, **Poems by Rachel Kellum**
(Released July, 2012)

Rachel Kellum's first published book is a transparent poetic odyssey into the ethereal that is both provocative and inspirational. With *ah* Rachel Kellum demonstrates a maturity of craft that bespeaks the power of poetry to suggest what logic always struggles to explain about our divine nature.

Catalyst, **Poems by Jeremy Martin**
(Released December , 2012)

This is Jeremy Martin's first book of poetry and is a mind field of delight. It explodes with incendiary insight, cosmic playfulness and dizzying joy. It lifts us up on the back of a rocket and leaves in the weightless orbit of inner self.

All Liquid Light Press books are available directly from *www.liquidlightpress.com* **both in print and as e-books or from any of the current major global distribution channels including Amazon, Barnes and Noble, the iBookstore and the Ingram Catalog.**

www.ingramcontent.com/pod-product-compliance
Lightning Source LLC
Chambersburg PA
CBHW021915040426
42447CB00007B/875